Brand Universe

A Big Idea Marketing Strategy

By Jerry Bader

MRP
WEBMEDIA

Written & Photographed by Jerry Bader
Photographic Model: Carol Cunningham

Preface
It's not what you know that counts; it's what you need to know.

Today analytics rule, and that approach may be just fine for some businesses; but as seemingly rational as number crunching may appear, it only tells you part of the story, and that can be misleading. Statistical analysis can tell you what people did, but it can't tell you why; and it doesn't tell you what they would have done if presented with an alternative. Even A-B testing won't provide the answer to why people did what they did. What gets lost in a mountain of data is markets are an audience, and audiences consist of people not numbers. It doesn't matter if you sell a product, service, or idea, answering the question why people should care about you, or what you sell, is critical to your success. The ability to connect to people on a human level is what marketing is all about. In short, marketing is a people problem, and you won't find the solution on a spreadsheet.

In today's highly competitive online marketplace with so many businesses selling the same, similar, or substitute offerings, the battle for competitive advantage is being fought on the brand-marketing front. Creating a brand universe allows you the freedom to be innovative in your communication efforts; it separates you from copycat marketers and price-cutting vultures intent on profiting from your hard work.

In "What's The Big Idea?" we discussed the problem from a big idea perspective because a big idea is how you differentiate yourself from the competition, but having a big idea will only be of benefit if it is implemented properly.

Developing a Marketing Strategy Using Brand Story

Every business has a personality whether you create it yourself or you allow your audience to create it for you. There is no doubt that in today's highly connected digital social media obsessed marketplace your audience has the potential influence to make you the next big thing or just as likely, twist your well-meaning efforts totally out of shape, making you an object of ridicule. In other words, abdicating the responsibility of managing your image, identity and brand to the open market can lead to the unintended consequence of misrepresentation caused by communication errors, omissions and misinterpretations, resulting in a public relation's crisis that may be both long lasting and financially disastrous.

Managing your business personality is more than having a Facebook, Twitter and Google account. These are merely tools that may or may not be appropriate or productive for your business, but before even considering what tools to employ, you need to decide what your business personae is going to be.

Managing your brand personality is deciding exactly who you are as a business. Once that is decided, the mission is to be as consistent as possible in the presentation of that identity. With a defined personality and a commitment to consistent presentation in all things marketing, you then can decide what tools you need to implement your strategy, whether they be Facebook, Twitter, Video, Print, Adwords, blogging, e-books, mobile or whatever else may be available.

Ideas To Spark The Imagination
Defining Movie Genres In Marketing Terms

Action

When the decision to buy depends on the audience taking aggressive action or the emotional value that prompts the purchase is founded in confronting a physical force then the Action Universe may be the right choice. Examples: gym memberships or physical fitness DVDs.

Do You Want To Be In Control Or Not?

The bottom line is simple: do you want to be in control of your image, identity and brand or are you willing to relinquish that responsibility to a fickle marketplace and unfettered social media platforms that have little or no oversight, allowing and maybe even encouraging the most extreme intemperate opinions to flourish; opinions that may be innocently uninformed or purposefully destructive, and ultimately dependent on and influenced by a small sample size of highly vocal self-promoting participants.

Your brand personality, in conjunction with your big idea marketing strategy, determines the tactics and tools needed to implement your action plan. "What's The Big Idea?" provides companies with twenty-eight concepts that can form the basis for developing a successful marketing strategy. Your big idea concept can either be determined by the brand personality you wish to implement, or direct you to the brand personality needed to support your big idea. This can be a tricky distinction. You may see your brand image through the myopic viewfinder of closeness, and like a lens with a narrow depth-of-field you may not see the whole picture in focus. Your big idea must be in sync with the brand personality you choose to present or you will defeat yourself before you even start.

Self Promotion Versus Brand Personality

Entrepreneurs and sole-proprietors have to be especially careful not to fall prey to over zealous ego-induced self-promotion that misrepresents the brand and the value it offers. Not every owner-manager is cutout to be a company's brand hero or audience surrogate. It can work and there are many examples of when it has, but first you have to ask yourself are you brand-hero or surrogate material? You may be smart; you may be skilled at what you do; and your spouse and children may think you're wonderful and witty, but that alone does not make you a brand hero or an audience surrogate. The question is, are you willing or capable of living up to what by definition is a stylized ideal in a highly opinionated, unregulated social media environment that calls for instant judgment and uninformed commentary often with venal intent?

Brand heroes are idealized notions that your audience can strive to emulate or associate with, but they are not real. Real people are complex and multi-dimensional; they have strengths and weaknesses and are accepted as such, but brand heroes are simpler, less complicated characters designed to focus attention on a core value. Brand heroes are hyper-real: in the same way that Alfred Hitchcock described movie scripts as life with the dull parts taken out, brand heroes are realistic but with all the messy, confused, contradictions real people carry as baggage removed for clarity's sake.

Associating management or ownership too closely with the brand personality can have unintended consequences, and you better never screw-up. When owner-managers mess-up publically the market takes it personally and forgiveness comes at a high price. That said, some kinds of businesses tend to gravitate to self-promotion, but as a company grows it becomes harder and harder to sustain that kind of strategy.

Ideas To Spark The Imagination
Defining Movie Genres In Marketing Terms

Adventure

When the decision to buy depends on the audience stepping outside their comfort zone and venturing into new and often scary uncharted territory, but where the emotional value outweighs the uncertainty, or when the uncertainty is the reward, then the Adventure Universe may be the right choice. Examples: safari type vacations, hunting or dating websites.

You Goof, You Lose

The problem with confusing and mixing self-promotion with brand personality is obvious for anyone who thinks about it. A cosmetic firm that sticks too long with an aging diva as brand hero can quickly find itself out-of-touch with its youth market. Or for example, take the public relations nightmare created by a senior executive of a fast-food chain for his public comments on gay marriage. People can have whatever opinions they want, but if you're a public representative with foot-in-mouth disease, you better understand the consequences and financial risk associated with making your opinions those of your company.

The bigger you are the harder you'll fall if you make a public relations faux pas, but you don't have to be a high profile nationally advertised company to get in trouble. Social media has created a forum for every "got-cha" style wannabe journalist, blogger busybody and axe-grinder to ruin your reputation and business. Even if you are a business of one, you must think of your company as a separate entity, that lives, breathes, and exists on its own. You maybe the asset your clients want, but you're still a part of something greater than yourself.

An appropriate, well-managed brand hero strategy conveys the image of a larger more substantial organization with an identity and personality separate from management. It is a strategy that helps protect and insulate your company from polarized public opinion and the vagaries of social media firestorms.

Create A Brand Universe

Think of your brand as a self-contained universe, an eco-system filled with all the necessary elements that make for success. It sounds complicated but in fact it is the opposite. By looking at brand in this way, you eliminate all the extraneous irrelevances that just get in the way of delivering your essential marketing message. You are creating a brand story, and just like the filmmakers of Hollywood, you have to create an environment where your story can exist, an environment that sheds the flotsam and jetsam of real life and focuses on the problems your solution resolves.

Business people like to keep all their options open, but when it comes to marketing that kind of loosey-goosey approach can confuse your audience, obscure your identity, and relegate your brand to the instantly forgettable. The goal is to create a universe that is consistent, sustainable, and focused on the clarity of purpose: the 'why' anybody should care what you have to say, and take seriously what you're selling. Within this defined context you have flexibility, but like the universe itself, there are laws that govern behavior, and those laws shape what, how, and where you present your material.

Understanding Brand Universe Structure

When you watch a movie like "Iron Man" you forget about how totally ridiculous the plot, premise, and characters really are; you suspend disbelieve, and buy into the concept because the screenwriter and director have created a complete

Ideas To Spark The Imagination
Defining Movie Genres In Marketing Terms

Comedy

When the decision to buy depends on the audience seeking enjoyment as the emotional payoff or where the product or service is generally regarded as taboo or not generally discussed in polite conversation then the Comedy Universe may be the right choice. Examples: OTC constipation medicine or condoms.

universe where even the most outrageous people and contraptions can exist. By the same token if you develop a consistent brand universe, you create an environment where you can state your case and bypass superficial objections, while informing, entertaining, and educating your audience on what makes your brand different and above all special.

The Brand Universe strategy cannot be viewed as just another advertising piece. This is a long-term approach that requires planning and persistence if it's going to work. Because of the increasing power of Web and Mobile video, we will concentrate here on the video elements needed to create your Brand Universe, but all aspects of advertising need to enhance and support the strategy, including print, packaging, store design, and customer relations. This may all seem obvious but many companies struggle with balancing all the internal pressures, interest groups, and stakeholders, making implementation difficult without management's concerted focused commitment.

Your Brand Universe is developed over time through a series of campaigns, each with a story arc composed of multiple episodes. And although we are basically talking about a video approach, the same would hold true for print, radio or any other media form.

A Historical Perspective

Much of what is hyped as hot trends in the news, blogs, and social media is actually manufactured misinformation, marketing propaganda masquerading as public relations in order to benefit the power players at the expense of small business. And the strategy doesn't stop at promoting product sales and manipulating stock prices; it also influences perception, altering belief systems and market action.

Perhaps a little history is in order. Edward Bernays is regarded as the founding father of Public Relations. He is credited with coining the term 'Public Relations' as a euphemism for commercial propaganda, a seemingly benign form of marketing, lacking the negative baggage of political misuse.

Bernays was Sigmund Freud's American nephew. He took Freud's theories of man's need to fulfill his subconscious desires and used them in creating successful marketing campaigns. He used these techniques to promote such diverse clients and products as Calvin Coolidge, Enrico Carsuso, Dixie Cups, Alcoa, Dodge Motors, cigarettes to women, and bacon and eggs for breakfast. He is also accountable for helping overthrow the democratically elected President of Guatemala, Jacobo Arbenz Guzmanon, on behalf of the United Fruit Company.

Major business interests understand the process involved in shaping audience opinion and preference, manipulating consumers to blindly tweet and text their commercial messages, promoting purchase behaviors on their behalf. It's not big brother small business needs to be concerned with, as much as corporate big money interests.

One of Bernays' most infamous campaigns was for the American Tobacco Company. In the 1920s it was taboo for women to smoke. George Hill, President of the American Tobacco Company figured the company was only getting half the

Ideas To Spark The Imagination
Defining Movie Genres In Marketing Terms

Crime

When the decision to buy depends on the audience needing to protect itself from some outside harmful influence or criminal behavior then the Crime Universe may be the right choice. Examples: burglar alarms or self-defense courses.

potential market for cigarettes because smoking was a male-only habit. Bernays was hired to see if he could come-up with a campaign that would change public opinion and get women to smoke. He hired A.A. Brill, a New York based Freudian psychoanalyst to analyze what was behind the desire to smoke. What he discovered was cigarettes were a symbol of male sexual power.

Bernays hired a group of young debutantes and asked them to pretend to be suffragettes. They were told to march in a New York City parade with cigarettes hidden under their dresses. On his signal they were to light their cigarettes in front of a crowd of photographers and newspapermen who were prompted to be there. Bernays publicized the stunt by telling the press that suffragettes were going to light "Torches of Freedom" during the parade. Hence forth, women associated cigarettes with women's rights and the taboo was broken.

Putting the Pieces Together

The public has been trained like circus seals to adopt every false premise and cockamamie notion that big business deems important to boosting their cause. People have been sold on the idea of multi-tasking, despite the fact that every credible neuroscientist on the planet will tell you that multi-tasking is a fallacy; our brains just don't work that way. We've also been convinced that young people have little or no attention span so we need to explain everything to them in 140 characters or less. This is just poppycock, and it flies in the face of human nature and a few thousand years of story telling. Young, and not so young adults sit for hours deeply engrossed in some digital role-playing game or sports simulation, and that involves intense concentration. The problem isn't attention span; the problem is boring and inane marketing. Do people get turned-off by rambling presentations, of course. That is nothing new, and you can thank in part the democratization of the Internet with its low cost of access, affording every diluted amateur, egotist, and wannabe, a worldwide venue from which they can bore, confuse, and mislead whoever stumbles by.

Perhaps marketers should learn something from the gaming industry, and it's not that each brand should add some kind of 'Angry Birds' clone to their website, but rather, the essence of what gaming developers know. Gaming is story telling. Role-playing games are stories, they are based on the classic hero's journey; and sports simulations are basically the same just encased in a different wrapper. As far back as Aristotle, people understood a story is the best way to communicate a message and Twitter hasn't changed that underlying principle one iota.

Turning Story Into Brand Story

Business marketing often suffers from premature climax, as unfortunate a circumstance in advertising as it is in the bedroom. The first lesson to be learned about brand story strategy is that each installment needs a beginning, middle, and end. Whether it's a joke, a webisode, or a commercial message, it must be set-up, elaborated, and concluded in order to create memory and prompt action.

The brand story strategy is an investment that takes time, patience, and commitment. To expect instantaneous results would be a false expectation; it does happen, but overnight successes are generally the result of years of hard work and experimentation. So without a firm commitment, there is little point in

Ideas To Spark The Imagination
Defining Movie Genres In Marketing Terms

Detective/Mystery

When the decision to buy depends on the audience needing to resolve some mystery that has become a source of discontent or frustration then the Detective/Mystery Universe may be the right choice. Examples: any self-help course or educational/training product.

wasting resources. And if you insist on reacting to every manufactured pop-culture media blitz, you will quickly burn out in a flame of exhaustion and frustration. But if you think you've got what it takes to commit to a strategy, then you need to know the fundamental communication elements, and how they impact tactical considerations.

The Message

Each aspect of a brand story strategy is important but none is more important than the message. We are not referring to promotional messages like buy now and get twenty percent off, or buy two and get one free; these are promotional messages not branding messages. There is a time and place for promotions, but they should be featured within the context of the brand story and not the centerpiece of it. Every business wants to sell as much stuff as quickly as possible, but as stated earlier, rushing ahead to the climax without an appropriate set-up and elaboration will result in your message being lost in a daily deluge of competitive noise.

In "What's The Big Idea?" we discuss Maslow's Hierarchy of Needs, the perfect place to begin discovering the core brand message you need to deliver. Start with the three fundamental questions that govern most everything we do. Will it hurt me? Can I eat it? Will it have sex with me? These three questions along with social, esteem and self-actualization needs form the basis of all human survival strategies. Defining your offering as an answer to one of these basic needs, gives it the gravitas to motivate your audience to act. It just doesn't get much more fundamental than that. In one way or another, every significant brand answers one of these questions; some like fashion, cosmetics, and health care are obvious while others like automobiles, software, and computers are disguised under layers of rationalization and justification, but a little imagination and thought will reveal the hidden psychological motivator.

The Medium

Video, audio, image, and copy each have their own set of required expertise and financial investment. What makes the Internet such an effective marketing environment is that each of these communication methods can be used separately or together, and the barrier to platform entry is minimal. The problem is how to use them effectively, putting a premium on multiple areas of high-level expertise demanded by ever changing, and increasingly technical, Web and mobile platforms.

The cult of amateurism that pervades the Internet due to the low cost of entry, plus a lack of business acumen created by an emphasis on technical solutions designed to solve human problems has led to a venue that breeds mediocrity and worse. More than fifty years ago Newton Minow, a former Chairman of the Federal Communications Commission, referred to television as a "vast wasteland:" you need to look no further than the plethora of pseudo-reality TV shows and one-hour programs that are forty-four minutes with the rest repetitive huckstering. So with fewer barriers to entry is it any surprise that the Internet has fallen victim to the same mindless infection of lowbrow programming and narcissistic self-indulgent marketing passed off as social media?

Ideas To Spark The Imagination
Defining Movie Genres In Marketing Terms

History

When the decision to buy depends on the audience getting in touch with their roots or where a historical event or character can serve as inspiration for resolving some emotional desire or physical need then the History Universe may be the right choice. Examples: political campaigns or establishment services like banks.

Granted, the Internet has produced some of the most imaginative marketing and communication examples from some of the best and brightest who otherwise may never have had a chance of accessing a market, but much of what is superlative gets buried under a mountain of mediocrity. A fact that is exacerbated by the public relations machines of big business that constantly manipulate the game, making sure they're on top; while allowing an occasional newbie a big pay day, creating the allusion of hope for the multitudes of wannabe nouveau entrepreneurs. The Internet is like a Vegas casino, offering you hope and riches while quietly picking your pocket of everything but the lint.

The solution, and yes Martha there is a solution, is knowledge, understanding, and education. No one can be an expert in everything. The increasing demand for psychological, creative, and technical expertise is staggering, and part of that expertise is to know how to compete without succumbing to amateurism or costly corporate competition.

The Audience

Companies like Google, and for that matter any company that sells ad space, sells their audience demographic: where they live, how much they earn, what education they have, etcetera. It's an easy sell because on the surface it seems logical; after all, you can't buy a six hundred dollar mobile phone if you don't have six hundred dollars. But is that really the case? Lots of people buy things that on the surface they can't afford, or spend money on luxuries and fantasies when limited funds could be better and more logically allocated.

That is not to say that demographic analysis is useless, like most things it has its place, but the more important aspect of audience is what psychological triggers motivate them to action. Rather than think in terms of demographics, I prefer to think in terms of the psychological makeup of people based on personality, preference, belief, and values. Is it really true in today's business environment that you can't buy a six hundred dollar phone unless you have six hundred dollars? Of course not, all you need is a small deposit and a pen to sign-up for a three-year mobile phone contract. How much you make may factor into the decision but the desire to have a phone with all the bells and whistles instead of something cheaper is determined more by self-image, desire, and preference rather than by someone's pay check.

We have already discussed the three basic criteria that motivate much of what people do, and those three fundamental questions can be expanded upon using Maslow's Hierarchy of Needs. You can make business as artificially complicated as you like, but in reality effective marketing is all about using psychological persuasion to tap into your audience's reptilian brain to trigger instinctive responses. If you can put aside all the confusing, contradictory media induced promotional hysteria that bombards us daily you'll then be able to psychologically define your market based on the hardwired motivational triggers that prompt behavior. Standard demographics don't answer all the right questions. The reality is people act to satisfy emotional needs and hardwired instincts, and that trumps price, features and the competition every time.

Ideas To Spark The Imagination
Defining Movie Genres In Marketing Terms

Fantasy

When the decision to buy depends on the audience craving escape from reality, or where the make-believe world better illustrates the emotional reward that can be achieved in the real world better than a boring real-world explanation, then the Fantasy Universe may be the right choice.

Examples: beauty salon services or clothing brands.

The Environment

Where are people going to see your presentation? Are they going to be on a bus surfing the net with their iPhones? Are they going to be at home in front of their fifty-inch television or twelve-inch laptop computer? The device being used and the environment within which the marketing message is being delivered, makes a difference. Take for example a family at home watching television in their living room. A fairly standard picture of domestic tranquility, but let's look a little closer into what actually is happening.

Mom wants to watch the latest episode of her favorite romantic comedy while Dad would prefer the new detective series. After a few meaningful glances, and some quiet give and take, the big screen is tuned to the romantic comedy with the promise of cops and robbers to follow. In other words, what to watch and when, on the big screen, high-resolution television with surround sound audio, is a negotiated settlement. At the same time, the teenage daughter is plugged into her iPhone with the latest pop star assaulting her eardrums, while her fingers tap text message after text message to everyone she knows. Similarly her little brother is deeply engrossed in the latest game app on his iPad, mumbling encouragement to his digital surrogate. The children may be in the same room as their parents but they are having a different experience: they are isolated and alone despite being surrounded by family, and they are deeply involved in a more personal, tactile experience. The presentation experience makes a difference, which is what Marshal McLuhan said when he coined the aphorism, "the medium is the message."

The Messenger

In the 1992 Robert Altman movie "The Player" a new studio executive, Larry Levy (played by Peter Gallagher), suggests that they are paying too much for scripts, and that anybody can put together a movie concept by just looking at the headlines in the paper; to which Griffin Mill (played by Tim Robbins), the executive in charge of hearing pitches and selecting writers, replies sarcastically, ..."an interesting concept... to get rid of the writer from the artistic process. If we can get rid of the actors and the directors, maybe we've got something."

The hardest thing about business, especially marketing, is dealing with people. If there's a problem, it generally revolves around people, whether staff, colleagues, suppliers, or customers, it always seems to be a people problem; but people problems are exactly what marketing is suppose to solve. Unfortunately the digital age has created the impression that people are basically nothing more than extensions of the technology they use; and that one-dimensional digital snippets of thought can easily replace articulate communication. Oh sure you hear a lot of gum flapping about conversations with your customers through social media, but who are they kidding? Social media, tweets, and boilerplate auto responder emails are not conversations. Marketing is not the sum total of your Facebook friends and Twitter followers, nor is it a digital bribe soliciting meaningless 'likes' in return for some usually worthless freebie.

Unfortunately, novice Internet entrepreneurs have succumbed to the hype and misinformation that surrounds social media. This new class of business deems

Ideas To Spark The Imagination
Defining Movie Genres In Marketing Terms

Horror

When the decision to buy depends on the audience's fear of some potential disaster or where safety concerns and wellbeing are paramount then the Horror Universe may be the right choice. Examples: insurance products or home alarm systems.

humanity too messy to deal with. If the golden boy creator of the social media phenomenon is anything close to what has been reported, is it any wonder his creation actually produces antisocial behavior. The best way to communicate a message is with a messenger, a real person who knows how to deliver a convincing performance and a persuasive argument that taps into the psychological triggers that create desire.

The Performance

I recently watched a seminar that purported to teach people how to be YouTube superstars. You would think based on the adulation extended to successful movie, stage, and television actors that people would have more respect for the skills and techniques required to be an actor, let alone the writers, directors, camera operators, audio techs, and the music and sound designers required to create a compelling memorable experience. Anyone can do that stuff, right? Wrong! The bogus promise of "Forrest Gump" that anybody can make it big-time is nonsense. Yet the Internet with all its great and vast potential has provided a platform for every charlatan and ego starved wannabe Tony Robbins, to peddle his package of false consciousness. No doubt there are some business people that have what it takes to be onscreen personalities, but these people are few and far between. The leveling of the Internet playing field has led to a cult of amateurism in search of celebrity, fostering the idea that anybody can do anything; a fine sentiment, but it just isn't realistic for the average Joe Doakes. Without a well-executed performance by your onscreen presenter, all the creative thinking, hard work and planning you put into your big idea will dissipate as quickly as the air escaping from a punctured balloon.

The Personality

The John Wayne, Gary Cooper, Clint Eastwood version of the American cowboy is as fictitious as John O'Hurley's version of J. Peterman on the "Seinfeld" television show. The American cowboy that most people know was fabricated by a handful of European immigrants who created the movie industry, men whose closest experience with a cowboy was a Cossack.

I cannot emphasize enough the importance of understanding how people process and retain information. Reality is just too damn messy and conflicted to keep straight, so we tend to simplify things. We create caricatures in our heads of people, things, and situations because caricatures emphasize the differences, the elements that standout. Those elements are the things we find easiest to remember. From a marketing perspective the real J. Peterman could never be J. Peterman the brand, but the actor John O'Hurley can and did. O'Hurley provided the personality, style, and connective subtext needed to sell the public on the company's brand story, and in fact the fictitious version of Peterman helped enable the refinancing of the company after it went bankrupt.

Being a nice person with a nice personality may make you a terrific friend or even a great boss or colleague, but that doesn't make you a brand hero or audience surrogate, nor should it. Your brand personality must stand apart so it can be maintained, sustained, and fostered over the long haul.

Ideas To Spark The Imagination
Defining Movie Genres In Marketing Terms

Romance

When the decision to buy depends on the audience's need to seek affection and companionship or where the desire to overcome loneliness is the emotional need being sought then the Romance Universe may be the right choice. Examples: dating sites or cosmetics and perfumes.

The Look

What you look like, the clothes you wear, and the environment you're in, all affect the conversation, and impact the meaning of the communication. In person, people filter out whatever seems irrelevant, and concentrate on the verbal and nonverbal signs that add significance and subtext to a conversation. Most people have an in-person presence that transcends what otherwise might be conflicting or confusing signals, but that in-person personae rarely translates into an on-screen presence. The same person that comes across as impressive, knowledgeable, and authentic in person might come across as ordinary, arrogant, and untrustworthy on video. The in-person and digital experience are vastly different. Controlling the digital experience is far more complicated than controlling the face-to-face experience.

The decision to use an attractive female or a rugged male actor makes a difference. The decision to dress an actor in colors that reflect the brand's logo or packaging makes a difference. The decision to shoot on a plain background concentrating attention on the speaker, or a complicated set with many moving parts makes a difference. The camera angle, the editing techniques, the lighting setup and on and on, all make a difference both in style and substance. Appearance matters: it's a tool you use to impart meaning, convey impact, and imbed memory. You can control content, context, and subtext, and make it work for you, or you can ignore it and have it work against you.

The Sound

Video can include many different media types: images, text, animation, voiceover, onscreen actors, music and sound effects, with each used separately, together, or in an endless variety of combinations. Each of these elements enhances the experience, and helps convey meaning, but without sound your presentation will be dead. How you use sound to present your message could be the one factor that turns a boring presentation into a memorable experience. Your edge is the fact that the average online company doesn't understand how to use sound effectively.

Sound is the most important but least appreciated and understood element in video marketing communication. Try watching a movie with the sound turned off and even if you can follow the plot, all the emotion, subtext, and meaning will be removed. Even in the early days of motion pictures before "talkies" moviemakers understood the need for a piano accompaniment.

There are at least four components of sound that can either contribute to or detract from presenting a credible presentation. The first element to consider is technical and environmental. The kind of microphones you use, where they are placed, what they are connected to and recorded on, the preamps in your camera, and the environment in which you are recording all make a difference in the quality of the audio. If you think it doesn't matter, you'd be wrong, especially if you expect people to shell out hard earned cash to buy whatever you're selling.

Ideas To Spark The Imagination
Defining Movie Genres In Marketing Terms

Science Fiction

When the decision to buy depends on the emotional value an audience receives from possessing the latest state-of-the-art technology and gadgets that promise future possibilities, or that fulfill previously imagined fantasies, then the Science Fiction Universe may be the right choice. Examples: electronics, software, phones, and medical research.

Voice is one of the most feature rich instruments you can use to deliver meaning and impact. The quality of the voice, the tone, pitch, cadence, and use of inflection all can be used to tell a story that infiltrates the deepest reaches of the mind because it forces the brain to paint a mental picture. If you search the Web for old radio story broadcasts or even the new Internet versions you will see how powerful voice can be. The impact of Orson Welles' 1938 radio broadcast of "The War of the Worlds" is still talked about today. Never underestimate the power of the human voice, as a means to connect with your audience.

And of course music creates the emotional subtext of a presentation defining how the audience interprets each scene, each point, and each change of mood. Slapping on some pirated tune or royalty-free ditty because you like it, without reference to how it affects the emotional impact of the presentation can be counterproductive if not totally disastrous. Music is emotion, it sparks attention, excites, calms, and prompts people to move, hopefully to move their mouse over to the buy button and click.

If voice and music deliver content, meaning, and emotional reference, then sound effects deliver emphasis. Music and voice are the language and grammar of sound design while sound effects are the punctuation: sound design emphasizes what needs to be stressed, and draws attention to what needs to be noticed. Sound design is your subliminal secret message decoder that turns words and images into meaningful communication. It can be the competitive edge you gain over your competition.

The Words

If sound is the most complicated and least understood element of communication, then words come a close second. Words have meaning. All animals communicate but only our species has the ability to use words to articulate the full scope, breadth and subtlety of meaning needed to survive and dominate in a hostile environment. What separates the winners from the losers is how we use words to communicate. The trouble is most people have no respect for words; people are lazy in their use of language. Perhaps it doesn't matter around the dinner table, but when it comes to communicating your message to the world, or even just your email list, you can't afford to be sloppy. When people say things like "so fun" they don't sound current or cool, they sound like inarticulate dolts. We all make mistakes, and everyone can be forgiven for misspeaking now and then, after all, we are all human, but language is far too important to ignore, abuse, and contaminate.

Language evolves, expands, and changes over time and that is something that we all must appreciate and accept, but words have meaning both literally and metaphorically. All language is a form of negotiation whether it's asking someone for a date, to pass the salt, or to buy your product. Ignoring the consequences of inarticulate communication is a serious business error. The current fashion of truncating everything to its Twitter or texting form is not efficient, nor is it effective, it's foolish. Without context, words can be easily misunderstood and meaning misconstrued. Stream-of-conscious emails without any thought to how the correspondence will be interpreted are self-defeating. It

Ideas To Spark The Imagination
Defining Movie Genres In Marketing Terms

Social Drama (Antiestablishment)

When the decision to buy depends on the emotional value an audience receives from going against the norm, in fighting the good-fight to achieve some personal or social benefit, freedom, or positive result, then the Social Drama Universe may be the right choice. Examples: socially conscious charities, political campaigns, or businesses that want to create a counter-culture or under-dog brand.

is said that Lincoln once remarked that he would have delivered a shorter speech if he had more time. Brevity and understanding come at the cost of the time spent perfecting clarity, but then the density of meaning can be too intense for a perpetually distracted audience. Isn't it time to grow-up and think like an adult rather than an adolescent with an undeveloped prefrontal cortex? If something is important to say, perhaps it's important to say it properly, and if it's not important, maybe it need not be said at all. In the long run that would save everybody time.

You might try listening to the dialog in movies like "The Maltese Falcon" or anything written by Aaron Sorkin or Quentin Tarantino. They are great examples of stylized human dialog with the dull parts taken out in order to perfect meaning. If you want an edge in a dog-eat-dog competitive world, learning how to use language to your advantage could be your golden ticket.

Your Big Idea As Metaphor

A brand story strategy is the creation of a corporate metaphor for why people need to buy what you sell. It's an extension of our earlier work "What's The Big Idea?" Together they form the basis for what will separate you from the competition. Done right, they provide a competitive advantage. They just might be the missing ingredients that make a difference.

It's one thing to understand these things intellectually but it's another to be able to put them into practice. You cannot be expected to know how to do everything, nobody can, but it is important to understand how these things impact your marketing communication and the perception of your brand, so when you hire marketing people, you know what to ask for, and to demand more than the usual statistical blarney that sounds good on paper but ignores the 'why people do what they do' factor

Putting The Pieces Together

Creating a brand story marketing strategy can seem like a daunting task and it requires a multitude of skills. We have tried to explain why you cannot solve human problems and satisfy human needs with technical tactics without reference to basic psychology. Technical tactics solve technical problems, but marketing requires something more fundamental than a cool app or a pseudo-social social media website. If you have the communication skills to inform, enlighten, and entertain an audience by tapping into their hardwired desires, you will be successful. Whether you intend to go it alone, or you decide to hire outside marketing help, it's important to keep the project on track and not to be led astray by trendy gimmicks. Below are five things to keep in mind when making your decisions.

A Development Check List

1. Find The Maslowian Need

Finding where on Maslow's Hierarchy of Needs your offering rests, answers the question why your audience will care what you offer. Nothing is more fundamental than answering why. Knowing the why will keep you on track so that each marketing decision you make has a chance to work.

Ideas To Spark The Imagination
Defining Movie Genres In Marketing Terms

Thriller

When the decision to buy depends on the emotional value an audience receives from the adrenaline rush provided by the product or service, then the Thriller Universe may be the right choice. Examples: fantasy sports camps, white-water rapid style vacations or products like motorcycles.

2. Every Strategy Needs A Big Idea

We've talked about the three questions that form the basis for what motivates people to act, to buy what you sell, and to remain loyal customers. In "What's The Big Idea?" we provide twenty-eight strategies you can use to form the basis for how to implement your marketing communication efforts. Branding demands consistency and your big idea will inform every decision you make on what tactics to use, and what tactics to ignore, in developing your brand story.

3. Mould Your Audience Surrogate or Brand Hero

Audiences need to relate to your company in very human ways, and if they can see themselves in your marketing communication they are more likely to give your brand a chance. If your audience can vicariously participate in your brand story through the actions of your brand hero, you will have captured their imagination and created a barrier your competition will find hard to overcome.

4. Create A Brand Universe

Every story, every product, and every service exists within a narrowly defined universe. That universe can be as outlandish or as conservative as fits the need being promoted, but like all universes they have laws that govern behavior and these laws demand consistency. The brand story concept forces you to obey the rules, and those rules will help keep you on target and avoid being sidetracked by short-term trends. Your big idea, brand universe, and audience surrogate brand hero together form the basis for creating a successful brand that will connect to your audience both in the long and short term.

5. Develop And Deliver Campaigns

It is vitally important to remember the difference between a strategy and a tactic. A marketing strategy is an overarching big idea based on some fundamental aspect of human nature, sometimes referred to as a 'high concept.' A tactic is a tool used to implement a strategy. You can waste a lot of money on tactics that may work for others, but if they don't enhance your big idea, they will be a waste of time and money, and will most likely muddle your message and confuse your audience.

If you think in terms of campaigns rather than advertising you will extend the life of each marketing initiative. If each campaign is structured around a story arc, it will be easier to create; it will be more likely to stay on target; and it will be more effective because each new communication builds on the last. This process helps maintain communication consistency as well as determining what works best, and what to do next.

A Counter-Intuitive Approach

The brand story marketing-framework is counter-intuitive to traditional business approaches. It is not based on statistical analysis of past behavior, surveys of what people think they want, or focus groups manipulated to arrive at predetermined conclusions. Thinking outside the box, or just plain thinking creatively, is not for everyone. It requires a real dedicated commitment, but that is a good thing for those willing to take the plunge. The fact that many

**Ideas To Spark The Imagination
Defining Movie Genres In Marketing Terms**

Disaster

When the decision to buy depends on the fear from some real or imagined disaster that prompts the need to protect oneself or family, then the Disaster Universe may be the right choice. Examples: life insurance or legal and accounting services.

companies just won't "get it" makes it even more valuable to those who do. Following the path least traveled is scary, but the reward might just be worth it.

Postscript

There's a reason movie genres exist: they are classic story telling scenarios that audiences can relate to on an emotional and psychological level. From a business perspective, viewing your potential clients as an audience shines a whole new light on the process of marketing. The traditional customer-supplier relationship is by nature adversarial: you have what I want and you're demanding a ransom in order for me to have it.

Viewing your potential clients as an audience changes that perspective. If you accept the idea of offering your audience an Emotional Value Proposition (see "What's The Big Idea?" for a further explanation) rather than a mere price-based value proposition, you've taken the first step in building a Brand Universe.

Even if you reject the Brand Universe concept, or you're just uncomfortable with taking the path least traveled, why not use the concept as a mental exercise. Ask yourself what genre best suits your company's marketing objectives? It just might provide you with a new approach to how you present your brand.

Using movie genres to create a Brand Universe may seem at first glance to be a bit offbeat, but it is founded in acknowledged psychological theory.

We are all players in a movie we call life.

"Script theory is a psychological theory that posits that human behavior largely falls into patterns called "scripts" because they function analogously to the way a written script does by providing a program for action.

Silvan Tomkins (http://en.wikipedia.org/wiki/Silvan_Tomkins) created Script Theory as a further development of his Affect Theory (http://en.wikipedia. org/wiki/Affect_theory) , which regards human beings' emotional responses to stimuli as falling into categories called "affects": he noticed that the purely biological response of affect may be followed by awareness and by what we cognitively do in terms of acting on that affect...

In Script theory, the basic unit of analysis is called a "scene," defined as a sequence of events linked by the affects triggered during the experience of those events. Tomkins recognized that our affective experiences fall into patterns that we may group together according to... the types of persons and places involved and the degree of intensity of the effect experienced, which... constitute scripts that inform our behavior in an effort to maximize positive affect and to minimize negative affect." -Wikipedia

Ideas To Spark The Imagination
Defining Movie Genres In Marketing Terms

Western

When the decision to buy depends on the need to

harken back to a bygone age of simplicity and

imagined macho heroics then the Western Universe

may be the right choice. Examples: pick-up trucks

or anything macho.

Ideas To Spark The Imagination
Defining Movie Genres In Marketing Terms

Erotic

When the decision to buy depends on the need to fulfill a sexual fantasy, then the Erotic Universe may be the right choice. Examples: lingerie, perfume or condoms.

Ideas To Spark The Imagination
Defining Movie Genres In Marketing Terms

Psychological

When the decision to buy depends on the need to
fulfill some psychological proclivity or to protect
oneself from some debilitating phobia, then the
Psychological Universe may be the right choice.
Examples: entertainment vehicles like movies,
television, music, or books and self-help services
and products.

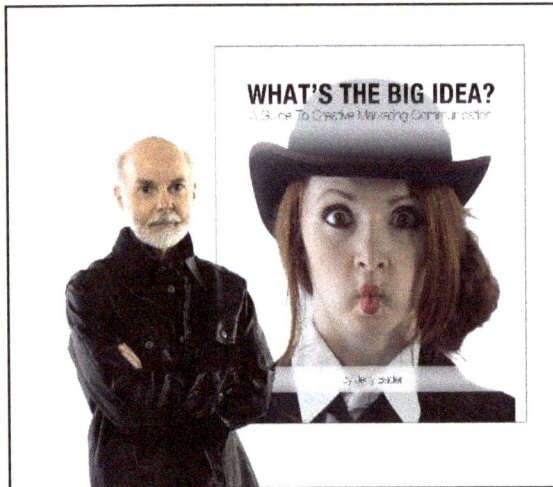

"What's The Big Idea?" is available on Blurb. com (http://store.blurb.com/ebooks/408096-what-s-the-big-idea) and on Apple's iBookstore (https://itunes.apple.com/us/book/whats-the-big-idea/id667106682?mt=11).

Ever Wonder What Make's People Tick?

We live in complex times, we have complex jobs, and our real and quasi-social relationships are as confused and frustrating as ever. So in a world of such complexity how can businesses truly understand what makes people tick? You may ask does it matter? And of course the answer is you bet it does. Without understanding how people make decisions and what motivates those decisions, you will not be able to connect with people, and failure to connect will severely hamper your sales efforts. Connecting with an audience is not so much about social media likes or pseudo friends, as it is about communicating your fundamental emotional value proposition in an articulate metaphorical manner.

The single strongest motivating drive that each person has is survival. In mans' early history, survival was almost exclusively a matter of life and death, but today that instinct has grown to include many aspects of both personal and business life. People are in a life long competition for food, money, companionship, knowledge, status, and personal perfection, all of which are filtered through the primitive reptilian brain's instinct for survival.

If you really want to connect to your audience, make sure your marketing strategy answers one of the three questions that form the fundamental motivating imperative of why people buy one product over another:

1. Will it kill me?
2. Can I eat it?
3. Will it have sex with me?

These seemingly simple, almost silly, questions are the essence of why, how, and what we do: from the tires we buy for our cars (will it kill me?), to the calorie-light dressing we put on our salads (can I eat it?), to the color of lipstick a woman uses (will it have sex with me?). Each decision we make boils down to the subconscious need to win the competition for survival both directly and metaphorically. Whether it's who gets the big contract, the corner office, or the pretty blonde, it's all about safety, well-being, and procreation, in short, survival. Business executives are trained to view the world from a perspective of cold hard facts, but somehow the cold hard fact of survival gets lost and confused by an overload of conflicting information and technical bafflegab that distorts, distracts, and prevaricates. When all is said and done everything boils down to the above three questions.

If you can creatively re-imagine your product or service to answer one of these questions, you will ultimately win the competitive battle for survival. If you would like to know just how we do it, we've created an e-book that contains twenty-eight concepts that can be used to reinvent your marketing strategy for the long haul. Viewing your business through the prism of one of these concepts might just be the secret marketing weapon you've been looking for. "What's The Big Idea?" is available on Blurb (http://store.blurb.com/ebooks/408096-what-s-the-big-idea) and on Apple's iBookstore (https://itunes.apple.com/us/book/whats-the-big-idea/id667106682?mt=11).

"What's The Big Idea?" contains 67 pages, a Concept Mind Map Chart, 28 photographic illustrations, text explaining the overall conceptual framework, a description for each idea, plus 29 videos (53+ minutes) further explaining the concepts. "What's The Big Idea?" was written by Jerry Bader, Senior Partner at MRPwebmedia, a marketing communication firm that specializes in Web video and audio production. He is the author of over one hundred articles on online marketing that have been published in various prestigious marketing blogs based on his forty plus years of business marketing experience. He can be reached at info@mrpwebmedia.com or mrpwebmedia.com.

www.ingramcontent.com/pod-product-compliance
Lightning Source LLC
Chambersburg PA
CBHW052339210326
41597CB00031B/5306